Mirror Series J

AN INTRODUCTION TO MODERN JAPANESE ORTHOGRAPHY: I *KANA*

Elizabeth F. Gardner
and
Samuel E. Martin

YALE UNIVERSITY
NEW HAVEN, CONNECTICUT

Copyright 1952

ISBN: 978-0-88710-039-0
YALE UNIVERSITY
NEW HAVEN, CONNECTICUT

PREFACE

The aim of this publication is to make information on the kana spelling system available to American students. Following the kana charts are graded exercises: they assume a knowledge of Japanese equivalent to the first half of Spoken Japanese by Bernard Bloch and Eleanor Harz Jorden (Henry Holt and Co., 1949).

For students who wish to be able to read older texts a sketch of old kana usage with exercises is included. This section is an attempt to take the place of George A. Kennedy's excellent 'Introduction to Kana Orthography', which is out of print.

AN INTRODUCTION TO MODERN JAPANESE ORTHOGRAPHY: I. KANA

0. Japanese may be written in romanization — that is, in Roman letters (Roomázi), in a syllabary (kana) which is like an alphabet but writes syllables instead of smaller units of sound, or in Chinese characters (kañzi). Until very recently, the Japanese have made little use of romanization themselves. There are several systems of romanization in current use, falling into two main types: the Hepburn type, which tries to write the consonants as in English and the vowels as in Italian; and the structural type, which systematizes the use of the letter symbols to correspond more closely to the structure of the Japanese language itself. The latter type is sometimes referred to as Nippoñsiki, and an excellent example of this type is the Yale system, a knowledge of which is considered prerequisite to the effective use of this book. Differences between the Yale system and other romanizations are summarized in Bernard Bloch and Eleanor Harz Jorden, Spoken Japanese 918-9 (Henry Holt and Co., 1949). The principal differences from the Hepburn system are the use of double vowels to indicate vowel length; the use of *hu* for *fu*, *tu* for *tsu*, *ti* for *chi*, *tya tyo tyu* for *cha cho chu*, *si* for *shi*, *sya syo syu* for *sha sho shu*, *zi* for *ji*, *zya zyo zyu* for *ja jo ju*.

1. Aside from books for children, very little is written with the syllabaries alone. The most common type of writing consists of Chinese characters mixed with the syllabary symbols: this is called kanamáziri. Another type of writing, very common in novels and some popular magazines and newspapers, consists of kanamáziri with the addition of reading aids in the form of kana alongside the characters to indicate their pronunciation. Kana used in this way is called hurigana and is printed in a reduced-size type known as rúbi 'ruby'.

2. When the kañzi were borrowed from China, the various writing styles of the Chinese were borrowed with them. There are three principal styles: the square-hand (kaisyo), running-hand (gyoosyo), and grass-hand (soosyo). These are sometimes compared to our block-printing, cursive writing, and shorthand respectively. To some extent this comparison is valid, but it should be remembered that the soosyo style has a high prestige

in the Far East, not for its speed so much as for its beauty. Writing is considered an esoteric art as well as a practical science. Proportion, stroke-order, and pressure are very important in executing a well-balanced character, regardless of the writing instrument. Soft pencil, crayon, or chalk are fair substitutes for the calligrapher's brush in reproducing the dynamic appearance of a well-written character.

3. There are two standardized kana syllabaries, katakana and hiragana. The Japanese derived both of these syllabaries from Chinese characters. In the case of katakana ('side kana') they took a side or corner from the square-hand form of the character, and in the case of hiragana ('smooth kana') they simplified the shape of the grass-hand form. In early Japanese writings the Chinese characters were often used themselves for phonetic values; such characters are sometimes called mañyoogana from their use in the Mañyoosyuu, an early collection of Japanese poetry. Often various characters were used to represent the same sound, apparently at the whim of the transcriber; sometimes, different characters were used for two different sounds which later fell together into one sound. As a result, when the Japanese began using the simpler forms of the characters for their phonetic syllabaries, they developed several rival symbols for the same sound. Eventually these variants were reduced to the standard sets we see today, though occasionally we find one of the less common older forms. These variant forms of the kana symbols are called heñtáigana ('queer-shaped kana'); some people take pleasure in using them in their own handwriting, especially when writing letters in the grass-hand style of calligraphy.

4. One of the difficulties posed by prewar Japanese texts was the vast number of characters in use -- from four to eight thousand. An equally perplexing problem was the large number of pronunciations represented by each of the characters. In an attempt to ease these difficulties, on 16 November 1946 the Ministry of Education (Moñbúsyoo) of the Japanese Government issued a publication called Tooyookañzihyoo 'Table of Characters for General Use' with a supplement Tooyookañzioñkuñhyoo 'Table of Sino-Japanese and Japanese Readings of the Characters for General Use'. These tables consist of a list of 1850 characters, with readings limited to those in common use; of these 1850 characters, 881 were selected as kyooikuyookañzi 'characters for educational use'.

It is perhaps still too early to say how successful these reforms will be, but there are indications that many Japanese magazines and newspapers are making an effort to conform to the new simplified standards. All government publications are supposed to conform by Cabinet order. In the postwar edition of the Naganuma readers (Naoe Naganuma, Hyojun Nippongo Tokuhon, Revised Edition, Tokyo 1948), the 881 characters for educational purposes are incorporated in the first four volumes, and the 1850 characters for general use are covered in the first six volumes. In addition, the first six volumes include 250 characters outside the standard list.

5. Through the course of their use in China and Japan, complicated characters were often reduced to abbreviated forms, particularly in hurried, everyday writing. These simplifications differed from the soosyo reductions, since the abbreviations were made by dropping or using a shorter substitute for some part of the character, instead of trying to capture the spirit of the entire character with a minimal movement of the arm. While the soosyo forms enjoyed a high prestige but were difficult to understand, the abbreviated forms (known in Japan as ryakuzi) were widely known, but considered vulgar. Since World War II the trend in Japan has elevated the status of the ryakuzi by standardizing the common written forms when these were simpler or more widely used than the printed forms. A list of the new standardized kañzi forms was issued by the Ministry of Education on 28 April 1949 under the title Tooyookañzizitaihyoo 'Table of Shapes of Characters for General Use'.

6. There has also been a reform with respect to the kana spelling usage (kanazúkai). The older spelling (kyuukanazúkai), sometimes called the historical spelling (rekisikanazúkai), was based on the etymological origins of the words. There have been several unofficial systems of new spelling (siñkanazúkai), also known as modern spelling (geñdaikanazúkai), each of which approaches the ideal of one symbol for each distinctive syllable.

As a supplement to the Tooyookañzihyoo of 16 November 1946, the Ministry of Edcuation included a chart of modern spelling under the title Geñdaikanazukaihyoo. The essentials of this system are summarized in section 7 below. The student should learn to write in this system, and then learn to read texts written in the historical spelling. He should bear in mind that there are other varieties of modern spelling. Most of those he will run across he will have no difficulty in figuring out for himself. The differences between the modern and the historical spellings are discussed in section 8 below.

In the tables of kana on page 19, Table 1 shows the hiragana arranged according to the traditional arrangement called the Gozyuuóñzu 'Table of Fifty Sounds' or just Gozyúuoñ 'Fifty Sounds'. The syllables are arranged in vertical columns (gyóo) corresponding to the initial consonant; the columns are named á-gyoo, ká-gyoo, sá-gyoo, tá-gyoo, ná-gyoo, há-gyoo, má-gyoo, yá-gyoo, rá-gyoo and wá-gyoo. The horizontal rows, for which there is no special term in Japanese (they may be called ráñ), correspond to the vowels of the syllables. In reciting the table, Japanese say it from right to left a column at a time as follows: aiúeo, kakikúkeko, sasisúseso, tatitúteto, etc. Since the symmetry of the table is broken by the lack of special symbols for *yi, ye,* and *wu,* the symbols for *i, e,* and *u,* respectively, are usually repeated in the appropriate boxes. The symbol for the syllabic nasal ñ (variously called by Japanese linguists hatúoñ, hanéru oñ, haneoñsetu, by others just ñ or úñ) is added at the end of the table. Table 2 gives the so-called dakuoñ 'voiced-initial syllables', which are written by using the appropriate symbol for the voiceless-initial syllable and then adding in the upper right corner two little strokes called nigoríteñ 'the nigorí (voicing) marker' or just nigorí. Thus *ka* with nigorí = *ga, te* with nigorí = *de, so* with nigorí = *zo,* and *hi* with nigorí = *bi.* In addition this table includes the syllables beginning with *p-* which are written by using the symbols for the corresponding syllables beginning with *h-* and adding in the upper right corner a tiny circle (drawn clockwise starting at the bottom) which is called hañnigoríteñ, hañnigorí or hañdaku, 'the half-nigorí marker', or maru 'circle'. The syllables beginning with *p-* are called hañdakúoñ 'half-voiced sounds'. This terminology goes back to various technical terms used by philologists in Ancient China and does not, of course, correspond completely to modern phonetic analyses of the language.

Since the syllabary provides no way of writing a consonant without an immediately following vowel, a spelling convention is used to write syllables beginning with consonant plus *y* (syllables called yóoon), such as *kya, kyu, kyo, sya, syu, syo,* etc. The consonant is given by a symbol from the *i*-row (*ki, si, ti...*) plus the symbol from the *y*-column having the required vowel, with the latter symbol written in reduced size and to the right. For example, *kya* is written *ki-ya, syo* is written *si-yo,* and so on. Writing the symbol from the *y*-column in reduced size and to the right prevents ambiguity between a syllable like *tyo* and a sequence of two syllables *tiyo*. These syllables with consonant + y are listed in Table 3.

To indicate the doubling of the voiceless consonants (pp, tt, kk, ss), another convention is used. The syllable *tu* is written in reduced size and to the right to indicate that the initial consonant of the following syllable is doubled. For example, hakkíri 'clearly' is written ha-tu-ki-ri, isséñ 'one Sen' is written i-tu-se-ñ, kitte 'stamp' is written ki-tu-te. By writing the syllable *tu* in reduced size and to the right, we avoid the ambiguity of a spelling i-tu-ka which might be either ikka 'how many days' or ituka 'five days'. Symbols written to the side may be referred to in Japanese as hazusita *ya*, hazusita *yu*, hazusita *yo*, hazusita *tu* (hazusu 'puts to one side').

Japanese grammarians refer to the syllable represented by the small *tu* as sokuoñ, tumáru oñ, or tumeoñsetu 'stopped syllable', i.e. syllabic consonant.

An example of both these spelling conventions illustrated in one word is issyo 'together' spelled i-tu-si-yo. Another example is happyakú 'eight hundred' spelled ha-tu-pi-ya-ku.

The student should learn the hiragana table first, in the conventional order of the Gozyuuoñzu. Table 4 is a rearrangement of the symbols according to their shapes. In the reading practices, the material is graded through each successive column of kana. The earlier exercises present single words and short phrases; later exercises include complete sentences. In the katákana exercises, some of the same material is repeated, but some new material also occurs. We have tried to limit the exercise material to expressions occurring in the first volume of Spoken Japanese, but in some cases we have used a few additional words.

Tables 5, 6, 7, and 8 show the katákana symbols in the same arrangements that Tables 1, 2, 3, 4 show for the hiragana symbols.

Except for use in children's books, government orders, and telegrams, katákana is largely restricted to spelling words of foreign origin such as náihu 'knife' (from English) and páñ 'bread' (from Portuguese), foreign and sometimes native Japanese proper names, words of lively or slangy connotation, and words having an exotic flavor. The katákana often seems to correspond to Western italics.

Although modern scientific books and some other publications are written in horizontal lines from left to right, most writing and printing is done in vertical columns (gyóo) from top to bottom, right to left. This means the page order in Japanese books is usually the opposite of the ordinary Western order; our last page is their first.

In earlier Japanese texts, punctuation was rarely used. Nowadays it is customary at the end of a sentence to use the period, made as a little circle at the right and bottom and called maru 'circle'. Occasionally within a sentence a comma is made as a short stroke to the right, called teñ 'dot' or 'mark'. The comma is sometimes also used alongside characters or kana to indicate proper names or special emphasis; a left-to-right diagonal stroke looking like a centered comma (\ ) is used to indicate the repetition of a preceding kana symbol (with or without an accompanying nigori marker). In both these latter uses it is called either teñ or tyoñ. A small plain dot is sometimes inserted between two kana symbols as a sort of separation hyphen; for example, between family and personal name when given in kana. A long line is used for a dash, and in the katákana spelling a somewhat shorter line is one way to indicate a long vowel (another way is by repeating the vowel). There is a long curve, which looks like the hiragana symbol for *ku* in an elongated form, and indicates that the preceding two or three syllables are reduplicated (as in nakanaka 'quite' mukasimukasi 'long ago'); this is called kurikaesi. If the repeated syllable indicated by the diagonal hook (\ ), or the first syllable of a reduplicated sequence indicated by the kurikaesi, requires a nigoríteñ or hañnigoríteñ of its own, this is added to the repeat sign or to the kurikaesi. There is also a sign indicating a reduplicated kañzi: 々 . Example: 人々 hitóbito 'people'. Two of these signs indicate reduplication of the preceding two characters: —人々々   hitoribítori 'one by one, one person after another'.

Other punctuation marks occur sporadically. For quotations, a slight half-rectangle ⌐ is made at the upper right, opening the quotation, and the other half-rectangle ⌊ is made at the lower left, closing the quotation. These symbols are called kákko 'brackets' or sometimes kagi 'keys'. Another type of quotation brackets are nizyuukákko 'double brackets' ⌐ and ⌊ . Ordinary parentheses, turned on their sides in order to fit the vertical columns, are called marugatakákko 'round-shaped brackets'; and square brackets, also turned on their sides, are called kakugatakákko 'square-shaped brackets'. A brace { or } , likewise turned on its side, is called oogákko 'large bracket'. Western style quotation marks (iñyóohuu) are

sometimes used. In vertically written texts side-lining on
the right (called yokósen or oosen 'side line') corresponds to
underlining, and instead of foot-notes (kyakutyuu) at the
bottom of the page, 'head-notes' (tootyuu) at the top of the
page are more common.

In most texts, spaces are not placed between words. In older
texts, there is no space even between sentences. In some
publications for educational purposes (e.g., the early selec-
tions in the Naganuma reader) spaces indicate words to be read
as a group.

Chinese, Arabic, and Roman numerals occur freely, and a mix-
ture of the Chinese digits from 1 to 9 with the Arabic zero is
quite common.

Most dictionaries and reference-books are indexed according
to the Gozyúuon table (*a, i, u, e, o, ka, ki, ku*...etc.), with
either no distinction being made between syllables with nigori
and those without (*ka* or *ga, ki* or *gi,* etc.) or with the nigori
syllables following in the case of specific homonyms (thus
the following order: tentoo, tendoo, dentoo, dendoo). The symbol
ñ often follows *mu*. Another way of saying the kana is the
iróha, which follows the order in which the kana were arranged
for an ingenious poem known as the irohauta which was so written that each kana symbol appears only once. Some older reference books are indexed according to this system. The iróha order
is as follows: i ro ha ni ho he to, ti ri nu ru wo, wa ka yo
ta re so, tu ne na ra mu, u wi no o ku ya ma, ke hu ko e te, a sa
ki yu me mi si, we hi mo se su.

7. In the 1946 spelling system of the Ministry of Education,
there are a few differences from what might be expected by
someone used to the Yale romanization. These are summarized
below. Note in particular the different treatment of *oo* in
hiragana and katákana. Exceptional cases are starred.

YALE	HIRAGANA	KATÁKANA
e	e	e
*Particle e 'to'	*he	*he
o	o	o
*Particle o 'direct object'	*wo	*wo
oo	o-u	o-o
*Oói 'is much', ookíi, 'is big'	*o-o	o-o
koo	ko-u	ko-o
*Kooru 'freezes', koori 'ice'	*ko-o	ko-o

YALE	HIRAGANA	KATAKANA
too	to-u	to-o
*Tóoru 'passes', tóosu 'lets pass', tooi 'is distant', tóo 'ten'	*to-o	to-o

(NOTE: All other consonants plus oo are written with the appropriate symbol for the consonant plus o followed by o in katakana, by u in hiragana. This means that hiragana writing does not distinguish koo 'thus' from kóu 'begs'. But see also section 10).

yuu	yu-u	yu-u

(NOTE: The verb meaning 'says' is pronounced yuu but written iu in both the Yale system and the new kana spelling, as a special exception.)

wa	wa	wa
*Particle wa 'topic'	*ha	*ha
zi	zi	zi
*Within a word, when zi is the voiced alternant of a basic ti as in tikazika 'very near', hanazi 'nosebleed', or when zi is a historically reduplicated and voiced syllable as in tizimu 'shrinks'	*di	*di
zu	zu	su
*Within a word, when zu is the voiced alternant of a basic tu as in kozútumi 'parcel', or when zu is a historically reduplicated and voiced syllable as in tuzuku 'continues'	*du	*du

NOTE 1: Except under the conditions given above for zi and zu, the symbols for di (nigori of tu) and du (nigori of zu) are not used. See also section 11. The symbols for wi and we are not used in this system at all, and the symbol for wo is used only to represent the particle o.

NOTE 2: The English sound in the first syllable of demon is sometimes shown by using the katakana symbol for de followed by the symbol for i reduced in size and to the right. In borrowed words like vaiorin (usually pronounced baiorin) 'violin', the sound v is sometimes indicated by using the symbol for u with the voicing marker (nigoríten) and writing the following vowel reduced in size and to the right.

NOTE: 3: Many Japanese make no distinction between *ee* and *ei* in their usual speech, but this distinction is maintained both in the Yale romanization and in the 1946 spelling system of the Ministry of Education.

8. Old kana usage (kyuukanazúkai) reflects an older stage of Japanese and, like the historical spelling of many English words such as *knee* and *knight*, no longer agrees with the pronunciation. These traditional ways of writing words are often met with on the printed page so that it is useful to be able to read them easily. Most of the conventions are limited to the *w* and *h* columns of the gozyúuoñ, and the rules of spelling are easier than for English.

The clue to much of the kyuukanazúkai is provided by the traditional way of writing the particles in the siñkanazúkai. The particle *o*, for example, is written with the kana symbol for *wo*, a syllable that does not occur in modern pronunciation. In any word in which *wo* is found it is to be read *o* (e.g. wo-ka = oka 'hill'). Similarly the symbols *wi* and *we* will always equal *i* and *e* (e.g. wi-ru = iru 'is', ko-we = kóe 'voice'). The symbol for *wa* is usually read *wa*; but the combination *ku* + *wa* is sometimes read *ka* and, with nigori, *gu* + *wa* = *ga* (e.g. ku-wa-si = kási 'cake', gu-wa-i-ko-ku = gaikoku 'foreign country'). Compare the convention of using the *i* row + the *y* column to represent a single syllable: si-ya = sya.

The particle *e* is written with the kana symbol *he*. This means that *he* has a double reading: either *he* or *e* (ko-ta-he-ru = kotaéru 'answers' he-ru = héru 'passes'). There are similar double readings for the rest of the symbols in the *h* column: *hi* = hi or *i*; *hu* = hu or *u*; *ho* = ho or *o*. The remaining symbol, *ha*, in addition to the double readings *ha* or *a* when it is not at the beginning of a word has a third reading *wa*. (Here again the particle provides the clue.) An example of this is ka-ha = kawá 'river'. The alternant readings of *h*-column symbols often appear in the forms of a consonant verb with a vowel before the final –*u* such as the word 'buys': ka-hu = kau; ka-hi-ma-su = kaimásu; ka-he-ba = kaéba; ka-ha-na-i = kawánai. (A rare reading of *hu* as *o* sometimes occurs, for example in a-hu-gu = aogu 'looks up to'.)

Summary:

Writing	= Reading	Writing	= Reading	Reading	= Writing	
wa	wa,(-a)	ha	ha, a, wa	a	a,(-wa),	ha
wi	i	hi	hi, i	i	i, wi,	hi
		hu	hu, u	u	u,	hu
we	e	he	he, e	e	e, we,	he
wo	o	ho	ho, o	o	o, wo,	ho
				wa	wa,	ha

There are also conventions for the reading and writing of groups of two symbols. (The reading of *ku-wa* as *ka* and *gu-wa* as *ga* has been mentioned already.) In siñkanazúkai the syllables *oo* are written *o-o* in some words and *o-u* in others, as in *so-u* = *soo* 'so, thus'. Any member of the *o*-row may be the first symbol of the combination. Another convention for representing *oo* in kyuukanazúkai is the combination *a-u* as in da-u-gu = doogú 'tools'. To these three ways of writing *oo* must be added the alternant vowel readings of the *w* and *h* columns. Of the possible combinations, only nine occur and not all of these are common.

Examples:
```
   o-o:  oho  : o-ho-ka-mi = ookami 'wolf'
         owo  : to-wo-ka   = tooka 'tenth day'
   o-u:  ohu  : ki-no-hu   = kinóo 'yesterday'
         wou  : wo-u-ze-i  = oozéi 'are many (people)'
         wohu : No common examples.
   a-u:  au   : sa-u-di    = soozi 'cleaning', to-u-ki-ya-u = Too-
                                                              kyoo
         hau  : ka-ha-u    = kaoo 'will probably buy'
         ahu  : mu-ka-hu   = mukoo 'other side'
         wau  : wa-u-zi    = óozi 'prince'
         wahu : No common examples.
```

When the syllables containing the *oo* begin with a consonant plus *y*, as in kyóo 'today', the old usage has a different convention. It uses the *e*-row plus *u* or *hu*; i.e., (C)e-u or (C)e-hu = (C)yoo. (C stands for any consonant.) For example, ki-ma-se-u = kimasyóo 'will probably come', ke-hu = kyóo 'today'. Similarly, but using the *u*-row (C)i-u or (C)i-hu = (C)yuu; for example, i-hu = yuu 'says', re-ñ-si-hu reñsyuu 'practice'. (This economical spelling can still be used in telegrams.)

Summary:

The syllables	oo			(C)yoo	(C)yuu
	o-o	o-u	a-u	e-u	i-u
	o-ho	o-hu	a-hu	e-hu	i-hu
			ha-u		
	o-wo	wo-u	wa-u		
		wo-hu	wa-hu		

The syllables *zi* and *zu* in new spelling are written with the nigori of *si* and *su*. But the nigori of *ti* is also read *zi*, and the nigori of *tu* is also read *zu*. In older usage, for historical reasons, the nigori of *ti* and *tu* are sometimes used, as in ózi 'uncle' and mizu 'water'. (Spellings such as de-u-ya-ku = zyóoyaku 'treaty', occur but they are rare.)

The doubling of the voiceless consonants in the new spelling is always indicated by *tu* as in a-tu-te = átte. But in older spelling *tu, ti, ku, ki* may indicate doubling. This occurs chiefly in compounds whose first member has a basic reading that ends in one of these four syllables. Since compounds are normally written with characters, in an actual text these alternant doublings are rare. Examples: ha-ti-hi-ya-ku = happyaku '800'; ga-ku-ka-u = gakkoo 'school'.

In general these older spellings appear only where there is a historical reason for them. Not all words containing, for example, (C)yuu are written i-u, any more than we write -ight for all words that rime with night. There is no way of predicting when a given convention will be used except by memorizing; and there is no way of distinguishing which way a given combination is to be read except by the context.

9. Inflected words are written with both kanzi and kana. The kanzi is followed up with okurigana 'send-off kana', to write the appropriate inflectional ending -- and, in the case of verbs of class II (consonant-stems), the last consonant of the stem as well, since the kana system never breaks a syllable into consonant and vowel. Thus to write a form like hanásu 'speaks', the character 話 takes care of the word through hana-, and -su is written in kana. To write a form like sírokute 'is white and', the character 白 is followed by the kana -kute. Also written in kana together with the ending is the last syllable of the alternant stems of the consonant verbs

-- like kái- from kák- 'write', hanási- from hanás- 'speak', kat- from kaw- 'buy', kát- from kár- 'mow, cut', isói- from isóg- 'hurry', asoñ- from asob- 'play', yóñ- from yóm- 'read'-- to which those endings beginning with t- (like -ta, -tara, -te) are attached. In the following forms, the part covered by the kañzi is given in brackets: [ká]ita, [haná]sita, [ka]tta, [ká]tta, [isó]ida, [aso]ñda, [yó]ñda.

Notice that the radical (or infinitive) form of vowel verbs (class I) has a zero ending, so no kana is written after the characters:

見に行きました   mí ni ikimásita 'I went to see'.

With consonant verbs (class II), the send-off kana is used if the form is really the radical (like yasúmi 'resting'), but not if it is a noun derived from the radical (like yasumí 'vacation'). Compare these sentences:

休みに行きました   Yasúmi ni ikimásita. 'He went to rest.'
休に行きました   Yasumí ni ikimásita. 'He went on a vacation.'

Sometimes old suffixes are written in kana after the character. For example, atarasíi is written [atara]sii. If there are several possible readings for the character, send-off kana may be used to help identify the reading:

下さる [kuda]sáru '[you or he] gives [you, me, or my family]'
下りる [o]ríru   'gets off'
下る   [sagá]ru   'goes down'

But okurigana does not resolve every ambiguous case. Only by context can you tell whether to read 上る as [nobo]ru 'climbs' or [aga]ru 'goes up'.

10. In Section 7, the rule for writing the sequence oo in hiragana was stated as o-u with a few exceptions written o-o. In addition to the exceptions given there, a few other words with the historical spelling o-ho are also often written o-o. And there are a number of compound words derived from the basic elements in some of the words like oói 'is many, is much' (basic element oo- 'to be great') which are also spelled o-o instead of o-u as you would expect from the usual hiragana rule. Here is a list of some of these exceptional words. The groups of derived words are not intended to be exhaustive, particularly not for oo-.

hóo		'cheek'
	hoobéni	'cheek rouge'
	hoozué	'supporting the cheek'
hóo	(no ki)	'*magnolia hypoleuca* (a kind of tree)'
hoozuki		'ground-cherry'
kooru		'freezes'
	koori	'ice'
moyóosu		'sponsors, gives (an entertainment)'
oói		'is many, is much'
	ooáme	'heavy rain, downpour'
	ooátari	'big hit, great success'
	oobúroshiki	'a big cloth wrapper'
	oogesa	'exaggeration'
	ooirí	'full house, crowded audience'
	óokami	'wolf'
	ookíi	'is big'
	oomune	'generally, for the most part'
	ooótoko	'tall man, giant'
	Oosaka	'Osaka'
	ooyake	'the public; the government'
	ooyoso	'roughly, approximately'
	ooyuki	'heavy snowfall'
oóu		'covers, wraps'
todokooru		'stagnates; is left undone'
tóo		'ten'
	tooka	'ten days'
tooi		'is distant'
	tooeñ	'distant relation'
	toonori	'a long ride'
tóoru		'passes through'
	toorí	'street, way'
	tooriáme	'passing shower'
	tóosu	'lets pass through'

11. In Section 7, the rule for writing the syllable *zi* was given as *zi* for most words, but *di* for a few words in which the syllable is an alternant of a basic *ti* rather than a basic *si*, and also for a few rare cases like tizimu 'shrinks' where the syllable *zi* represents a historical reduplication and voicing. Here is a list of compound words which have a *zi* that is an alternant of a basic *ti*, together with the basic element from which they are derived. In addition there are a very few examples of the syllables *zya* and *zyo* clearly alternants of basic *tya* and *tyo*. These are written *di-ya* and *di-yo*. (i.e. the nigorí of *ti + ya*

and + *yo*). There is at least one example of *zyu:* the suffix -zyuu meaning 'throughout' (itiniti-zyuu 'all through the day') which is derived from the element tyuu 'inside'. The examples of *dya* = *zya, dyo* = *zyo, dyu* = *zyu* are rare in actual texts, since elements containing these sounds are of Chinese origin and are usually written in kañzi.

ti		'blood'
	hanazi	'nosebleed'
tié		'wisdom'
	irezie	'suggestion, hint'
	saruzie	'shallow cunning'
	waruzié	'wiles, cunning'
tiká(i)		'(is) near'
	hasizika	'near the edge'
	mázika	'nearby, near at hand'
	tezika	'nearby, near at hand'
tikara		'strength'
	bakazîkara	'brute force'
tirasi		'scattering'
	matubazírasi	'a kind of design with pine-leaves'
	moñzírasi	'a kind of design with figures'
tirimeñ		'crepe'
	hizirimeñ	'scarlet silk-crepe'
tití		'milk; breast'
	moraiziti	'being nursed; receiving milk'
tyawañ		'bowl'
	teñmokuzyáwañ	'a kind of bowl'
	tyanomizyáwañ	'tea-bowl, tea-cup'
tyoosi		'pitch, tune'
	uwazyóosi	'high pitch, higher key'
tyootiñ		'paper lantern'
	yumiharizyóotiñ	'paper lantern with a bow-handle'

Just as *zi* is sometimes written *di*, the syllable *tu* is sometimes written *du*. A few examples of this were given in Section 7. Here is a longer list, together with the basic forms from which the words are derived:

tú		'port'
	tokiwazu, tokiwazubusi	'[name of a school of zyooruri (dramatic ballad)]'
túe		'stick, prop'
	hoozué, hoozúe	'supporting the cheek'

	ikizúe	'palanquin-bearer's staff'
tuká		'knife handle, hilt'
	kozuka	'knife worn in sword sheathe'
tuká		'mound, grave'
	hiyokúzuka	'double grave for young lovers'
	hurúzuka	'old mound'
	kaízuka	'shell heap'
tukae		'serving'
	miyazúkae	'the Court service'
tukai		'using'
	hitozúkai	'using employes, working one's men'
	kózukai	'servant, messenger-boy'
	kanazúkai	'kana spelling'
tukámi		'grasping'
	tezúkami	'grasping with one's fingers'
	wasizúkami	'eagle's grasp; grab'
tukari		'getting wet'
	mizuzúkari	'getting wet (with water)'
tukaré		'weariness'
	kizúkare	'mental fatigue'
	tabizúkare	'weariness during a trip'
tuke		'pickling'
	kasuzuke	'things pickled in rice-wine lees'
	misozuke	'things pickled in miso [bean-paste]'
	nazuké	'pickled vegetables'
tukéru		'attaches, brings in contact'
	kotozuké	'delivering a message'
	nazukéru	'names, designates'
tukí		'pounding in a mortar'
	tiñzukí	'pounding rice for wages'
tukí		'moon, month'
	házuki	'(Leaf-Month =) August'
	mi(k)kazuki	'3-day moon, new moon'
	nikúzuki	'(Meat-Moon =) name of graph radical 130'
	yoizuki	'evening moon'
	yumiharízuki	'crescent moon'
tukú		'contacts, adheres'
	dokuzúku	'spits venom, swears (at)'
	eñzúku	'(a woman) marries'
	kañzúku	'suspects, gets wind of'

15

	motozúku	'is based (on)'
	kizúku	'notices, perceives'
	tikazúku	'approaches, gets acquainted'
	tikarazúku	'by sheer force'
	tyoosizúku	'is high-spirited, lets go'
tuku-		'(exhaustive)'
	tukuzúku	'thoroughly, utterly'
tukue		'desk, table'
	kyoozúkue	'Buddhist scripture table'
	humizúkue, huzúkue	'book table'
	zimuzúkue	'business desk, office desk'
tukurí		'right-hand element in a Chinese graph'
	husizúkuri	'[name of graph radical 26]'
	onozúkuri	'[name of graph radical 69]'
	hudezúkuri	'[name of graph radical 129]'
tukurói		'repairs, adjustment'
	mizúkuroi	'dressing'
tukúsi		'endeavoring; exhausting (effort)'
	geizúkusi	'(extending) entertainment'
	kokorozúkusi	'kindness, attentions'
túma		'wife'
	hitozuma	'(another's) wife'
	niizuma	'newly-wed wife'
tumá		'skirt'
	hidarizuma	'left (front) skirt'
	kasanezúma	'wearing multiple skirts'
tumáru		'is obstructed'
	ikizumáru	'is choking, oppressing'
	yukizumáru	'comes to a standstill, deadlock'
tumé		'canning; canned goods'
	kañzumé	'canned food'
	orizumé	'food packed in a chip-box'
	susizumé	'canned food pickled in salt or vinegar'
tume		'nail, claw'
	kotózume	'pick used to pluck the strings of the kóto'
	namazumé	'the quick (of a fingernail)'
túne		'always'
	tunézune	'always; usually'

tunó		'horn'
	kozuno	'little horn'
	sikázuno	'deer horn'
turá		'surface, face'
	buttyoozura	'scowl, sullen expression'
	nózura	'surface of a plain; natural table; impudence'
turai		'tough, painful'
	kikizurai	'painful to hear'
	yomizurai	'painful to read'
	yarizurai	'painful to give'
turé		'accompaniment; companion'
	hutarízure	'a couple, party of two'
	michizuré	'traveling companion'
	otokózure	'male escort'
	tabizuré	'traveling companion'
	turézure	'leisure hours, time to kill'
turi		'fishing'
	okazuri	'fishing from the bank'
	tomozuri	'fishing with live decoys'
	yózuri	'night fishing'
turú		'string'
	yumízuru	'bowstring'
turú		'handle'
	nabézuru	'pot-handle'
turú		'vine'
	imozuru	'sweet-potato vines; pull, drag'
	tézuru	'interest, influence'
túru		'crane (bird)'
	orízuru	'a kind of crane'
tuté		'mediary'
	hitozute	'hearsay'
	kotozuté	'delivering a message'
tutí		'hammer'
	aizutí	'(hammers hitting together =) 2 people saying the same thing at the same time'
	kózuti	'small hammer'
tutó		'straw-wrapper; present'
	iézuto	'a souvenir for home'
	warazuto	'straw-wrapper'
tutomé		'employee'
	kaisyazútome	'company employee'

tutu		'tube; gun'
	kozutu	'rifle'
	oozutu	'cannon'
	tyazutu	'tea-can'
tutumí		'package'
	kozútumi	'parcel'
	komozútumi	'package wrapped in straw-mat'
tuyói		'is strong'
	kizuyoi	'is reassuring, encouraging'
	tikarazuyói	'is reassuring'

The lists in this section and the preceding section are given for reference purposes only. In compiling them, reference was made to the lists contained in a publication of the Asahi newspaper company: Asahi-siñbuñ-zyooyoo: Tooyoo-kañzi, geñdai-kanazukai, iikae-syuu [Characters for General Use, Modern Kana Spelling, and Paraphrases: For Regular Use in the Newspaper Asahi], Osaka, 1947.

KANA TABLES

TABLE 1

ñ	W-	R-	Y-	M-	H-	N-	T-	S-	K-	
ん	わ	ら	や	ま	は	な	た	さ	か	あ *a*
ゐ	り	(い)	み	ひ	に	ち	し	き	い *i*
(う)	る	ゆ	む	ふ	ぬ	つ	す	く	う *u*
ゑ	れ	(え)	め	へ	ね	て	せ	け	え *e*
を	ろ	よ	も	ほ	の	と	そ	こ	お *o*

TABLE 2

P-	B-	D-	Z-	G-	
ぱ	ば	だ	ざ	が	*a*
ぴ	び	ぢ	じ	ぎ	*i*
ぷ	ぶ	づ	ず	ぐ	*u*
ぺ	べ	で	ぜ	げ	*e*
ぽ	ぼ	ど	ぞ	ご	*o*

TABLE 3

ry-	py-	by-	hy-	ny-	ty-	zy-	sy-	gy-	ky-	
りゃ	ぴゃ	びゃ	ひゃ	にゃ	ちゃ	じゃ	しゃ	ぎゃ	きゃ	*a*
りゅ	ぴゅ	びゅ	ひゅ	にゅ	ちゅ	じゅ	しゅ	ぎゅ	きゅ	*u*
りょ	ぴょ	びょ	ひょ	にょ	ちょ	じょ	しょ	ぎょ	きょ	*o*

TABLE 4

こ	ko	す	su	む	mu	よ	yo	わ	wa	ん	n̄
て	te	さ	sa	を	wo	り	ri	れ	re	え	e
ひ	hi	ち	ti	ふ	hu	に	ni	ね	ne	う	u
そ	so	あ	a					ぬ	nu	ら	ra
ろ	ro	お	o	き	ki	け	ke	め	me	つ	tu
る	ru	せ	se	ま	ma	は	ha	の	no	く	ku
ゐ	wi	や	ya	も	mo	ほ	ho			へ	he
み	mi	た	ta			ゆ	yu			か	ka
ゑ	e	な	na	し	si						
				と	to						

TABLE 5

n̄	W-	R-	Y-	M-	H-	N-	T-	S-	K-	
ン	ワ	ラ	ヤ	マ	ハ	ナ	タ	サ	カ	ア	a
	ヰ	リ	(イ)	ミ	ヒ	ニ	チ	シ	キ	イ	i
	(ウ)	ル	ユ	ム	フ	ヌ	ツ	ス	ク	ウ	u
	ヱ	レ	(エ)	メ	ヘ	ネ	テ	セ	ケ	エ	e
	ヲ	ロ	ヨ	モ	ホ	ノ	ト	ソ	コ	オ	o

TABLE 6

P-	B-	D-	Z-	G-	
パ	バ	ダ	ザ	ガ	a
ピ	ビ	ヂ	ジ	ギ	i
プ	ブ	ヅ	ズ	グ	u
ペ	ベ	ヂ	ゼ	ゲ	e
ポ	ボ	ド	ゾ	ゴ	o

TABLE 7

ry-	py-	by-	hy-	ny-	ty-	zy-	sy-	gy-	ky-	
リャ	ピャ	ビャ	ヒャ	ニャ	チャ	ジャ	シャ	ギャ	キャ	-a
リュ	ピュ	ビュ	ヒュ	ニュ	チュ	ジュ	シュ	ギュ	キュ	-u
リョ	ピョ	ビョ	ヒョ	ニョ	チョ	ジョ	ショ	ギョ	キョ	-o

TABLE 8

ニ ni	ア a	コ ko	ナ na	ワ wa	ウ u	ノ no
テ te	マ ma	ユ yu	オ o	レ re	ネ ne	ハ ha
ラ ra	ヤ ya	ヨ yo	ホ ho	リ ri	ン n̄	イ i·
ヲ wo	セ se		サ sa	ト to	ソ so	メ me
エ e	ヱ e	ヘ he	キ ki	ロ ro	ツ tu	ル ru
モ mo		フ hu	ヰ wi		シ si	ケ ke
	ム mu	ス su			ミ mi	ク ku
ナ	ヒ hi	ヌ nu				タ ta
	カ ka					チ ti

STROKE ORDER CHARTS

Note: The charts on the following double page (read left to right) show the order in which the strokes should be made for each kana symbol--both hiragana and katakana. Some strokes are broken up only to indicate direction but should be made as smooth continuous curves in actual practice. In general, straight strokes are made from left to right or top to bottom and curved strokes frequently start at the top. (The charts are reproduced from George A. Kennedy's 'Introduction to Kana Orthography'.)

あ〜すあ	ち〜ちち	む〜すむ
いいい	つつ	めいめ
うﾞう	て〜て	ももも
えﾞうえ	とヽと	や〜やや
お〜すおお	な〜ナたな	ゆゆゆ
かワカか	にいに	よﾞよ
き〜きき	ぬいぬ	らﾞらら
くく	ねⅠれね	りりり
けⅠけけ	のノの	る〜るる
こﾞこ	はいには	れⅠれれ
さ〜さ	ひﾞひひ	ろ〜るろ
しし	ふﾞうふふ	わⅠわわ
す〜すす	へへ	ゐﾞゐゐ
せ〜せせ	ほいにほ	ゑ〜ゑゑ
そﾞそそ	ま〜まま	を〜すをを
た〜ナたた	みﾞみみ	んⅠん

ア フ ア	チ ー ニ チ	ム ユ ム
イ ノ イ	ツ ゛ ゛ツ	メ ノ メ
ウ ゛ ゛ウ	テ ー ニ テ	モ ー ニ モ
エ ー ㄒ エ	ト 丨 ト	ヤ フ ヤ
オ ･･ ナ オ	ナ ー ナ	ユ コ ユ
カ フ カ	ニ ー ニ	ヨ フ ヲ ヨ
キ ー ニ キ	ヌ フ ヌ	ラ ー ラ
ク ノ ク	ネ ゛ ヲ ネ	リ 丨 リ
ケ ノ ト ケ	ノ ノ	ル ノ ル
コ フ コ	ハ ノ ハ	レ レ
サ ー 十 サ	ヒ ノ ヒ	ロ 丨 ロ ロ
シ ゛ ゛シ	フ フ	ワ 丨 ワ
ス フ ス	ヘ ヘ	ヰ ー 丁 エ ヰ
セ フ セ	ホ ー ナ オ ホ	ヱ ー ア ヱ
ソ ゛ ソ	マ フ マ	ヲ ー ニ ヲ
タ ノ ク タ	ミ ゛ ゛ミ	ン ゛ ン

Note: The kana exercises and texts are arranged as they would be in a Japanese book; that is, they begin at what from the English point of view is the back of the book, and the pages are numbered accordingly.

dai-	big
mónzi	character, letter (also: mózi)
ii = itte	
hí o taku	kindles a fire
myoohoo	the supreme law of Buddha
ari = atte	
...no tóori ni	like...
taki = taite (taku)	
torii	gate of a shrine, a torii
issei ni	simultaneously, all together
tomósu	burns, lights
sizumi = sizunde	sinking
makká	very red, crimson
moe = moete (moeru)	
Kamogawa	P.N.
kawara	river beach, dry river bed
náku = nákute	
haruka	far-off
átari	neighborhood, environs
késiki	sight, scene, view
ni tótte	for, to (taking in)
minogasu	overlooks, misses, fails to see
méibutu	attraction (famous thing)

27. Kyóoto no okuríbi

Kyootó-si wa sihóo o yamá de kakomárete imasu. Higasigawa ní wa sáñzyuu rokú no yamáyama ga zutto tuzuite ori, kitá ni mo nisi ní mo sorézore yamá ga arimasu. Higasi no yamá o 'Higasiyama', kita no yamá o'Kitayama', nisi no hóo no yamá o 'Nisiyama' to iimasu. Maineñ hatigatu zyúugoniti ni wa koréra no yamáyama ni iroiro na katati no hí ga tukú no de yuumei desu. Kore wa búkkyoo no deñsetu kara kitá mono de, maineñ hatigatu tooka-góro kara sorézore no ie no goséñzo ni támasii ga hurúi ié ni káette kite, kázoku to issyo ni ituka no aida iru kotó ni nátte ori, hatigatu no zyúugoniti ni hutatabi koréra no támasii wa hotoke-sáma no tokoro e káette iku kotó ni nátte imasu. Kono káette iku támasii o okurú no ga, kono yamáyama ni tukú 'okuríbi' desu. Higasi-yama no naka no hitótu o 'Daimoñziyama' to ii, hyakumeetoru gúrai no óokisa no 'dái' no zi no katati ni, hí o takimasu. Kitayama ní wa 'Myoohoozañ, to iu yamá ga ári, 'myoohoo' to iu zí no tóori ni hí o taki, sonó hoka ni húne no katati, Nisiyama ní mo hitótu 'dái' no zi, 'torii' no katati nádo, miñna de itútu no zí ya katati no hí ga issei ni tomosare-masu. Hi ga Nisiyama ni sizumi, tyoodo hatizi-góro kara itizíkañ bakari no aida, Kyóoto no sóra wa makká ni moe, matizyuu no hitóbito wa kono hí o míru tame ni, mati no mañ-naka o nagárete iru 'Kamogawa' no kawara e dekákete ikimasu. Kyóoto no hito dake de náku, kono hí ni wa hárubaru Oosaka, Kóobe wa motíroñ, Tookyoo Yokohama átari kara mo kono utu-kusii késiki o mí ni takusáñ no hito ga atumátte kimasu. Nihóñ ni iru gaikoku no hitó ni tótte mo, kore wa minogasu koto no dekínai méibutu no hitótu desu.

Vocabulary for Exercise 27

okuríbi (okuri sending, escorting + hí, fire)	bonfire for speeding the spirits of the dead
sihóo	the four directions
kakómu	surrounds, encircles
ori = otte	
sorézore	each one
hí ga tuku	fires are lighted
deñsetu	tradition
goséñzo	ancestors
támasii	souls
hutatabi	again (a second time)
hotoké, hotoke	Buddha

25.

tooka	10 days, 10th day	kookoku	advertisement
óokami	wolf	mukoo	other side
ookata	for the most part	bínboo	poverty
kinóo	yesterday	hooritu	law
yooka	8 days, 8th day	tyootyoo	butterfly
Tároo	Taro	ikimasyóo	let's go
ikoo	will probably go	kyóo	today
byooki	sickness	simasyóo	will probably do
daróo	is probably	tyuumoñ	order
hañtoo	peninsula	yuubiñ	mail
zyoobu	health, safety	Hóñsyuu	Honshu

26. (Includes only words not in exercises 24, 25.)

arukimasyóo	will probably walk
gaikoku	foreign country
hanasimasyóo	will probably talk
iu	says
kási	cake
kimasyóo	will probably come
máiru	(humble) comes, goes
mawari	surroundings
mezurasíi	strange
myóoniti	tomorrow
nañzi	thou, thee
Níkkoo	P. N.
oozéi	crowd (of people)
óozi	prince
owari	end
ozi	uncle
reñsyuu	practice
sió	salt
soozi	cleaning
súzi	line
syoogatú	Jan., the New Year
Tookyoo	Tokyo
ueki	garden plant
ziyúu	freedom

ságeta mama	just as he was, after putting [it] down
buzi ni	without incident, safely
sore kara noti	after that
suteru	abandons
sutete oite	abandoning, leaving abandoned
nigéru	flee, run away
okutte morau	gets taken home, receives the favor of his escorting
gúrai	extent, pass, case
gúrai nara	if it comes to, if it's a case of
añsiñ	safety, security
káetta hoo ga añsiñ da (dá) soo desu	it's safer to return she says

24.

inaka	country		kaimásu	buys
ído	(a) well		tenugui	hand towel
táii	captain		atai	price
kurai	rank		áu	meets
iru	is		warau	laughs
kóe	voice		haráu	pays
é	picture		omóu	thinks
tukue	desk		arau	washes
éñ	yeñ		ié	house
túe	stick		káeru	returns
otokó	male		máe	front
oka	hill		kotaéru	answers
aói	is blue, green		áeba	if ... meets
oñná	female		kao	face
odoru	dances		yaoya	grocer, grocery
kaisya	(business) company		naósu	fixes
kázi	fire		ikiói	force, spirit
gañzitu	New Year's Day		nióu	smells, is fragrant
éiga	movie		zisiñ	earthquake
kawá	river		huzi	wistaria
kawanai	doesn't buy		tozíru	closes
niwa	garden		mizu	water
iwanai	doesn't say		sízuka	quiet
kawaru	changes		hazukasíi	is ashamed, shameful
aida	interval, space			
tiisái	is little, small			

kikoeru	is heard
kikoeta monó desu kara (= kikoeta kara)	
kosi	waist, loins
nukasu	omits, leaves out
kosi o nukasañ (= nukasoo)	will probably lose one's legs, collapse from fright
odoroku	is surprised, is amazed; is frightened
kosi o nukasañ bákari ni odoroku	are so scared they are about to collapse
omówazu	without thinking, unconsciously (negative adverbial)
kyá!, kyáa!	(shriek, scream)
oogóe o ageru	raise a loud voice
tamaranai	is unbearable, unendurable
motomoto	by nature
kowagáru	is afraid, is timid
kowagarí	timidity, cowardice
hotte oku	leaves alone, neglects
itimókusañ ni	at full speed, lickety-split
hasíru	runs
hasiri-dásu	starts to run, takes off
omáwari-sañ	cop, policeman
sirabéru	check up, look into, make inquiries
ittai náni	what on earth
sappári	(not) at all, (not) in the least
yokuyoku	very carefully, elaborately
irete átta	which had been put in (cf. Spoken Japanese 252-3.)
mezamasi-dókei	alarm clock
notta monó desu kara (= nottá kara)	because she had gotten on
botañ	button
tomeru	stop, turn off, shut off
nari-dásu	starts to ring
wasureru	forgets
ire (= irete)	puts in and
sono mama	just as is, just as it was
sukkári	completely
awatemono	scatterbrain, absent-minded person
warau	laughs

tokoro ga	but
tañzyóobi	birthday
iwái, oiwai	party, celebration
omaneki simásita (humble for manekimásita)	I invited
manéku	invites
-kuñ (= -sañ)	Mr. (familiar)
Yasui-sáñtati	the Yasui's, Mr. and Mrs. Yasui
nâkatta tame (= nâkatta kara)	because there wasn't
tyokusetu ni	directly
kabañ	suitcase
sagéru	sets down, puts down
yatte kúru	comes around, comes over
gotisoo	refreshments; meal
utá o utau	sings songs
géemu	games
tanosíi	is pleasant, is fun
asóbi (= asóñde)	plays and, played and (literary use of radical for gerund at the end of a clause)
sorézore	respectively, variously (each to his own)
miti	road
kurai	is dark
hitoribítori	one by one, one after another
(hito o) okuru	see a person off, see a person home
otaku (= uti)	house (honorific)
Gósyo	Imperial Palace (in Kyóoto)
yoko	side
hanasinágara	while talking (radical + -nágara 'while ...ing')
makkura (na)	is pitch-black
kurayami	darkness; dark place
suru to	and then
totuzeñ	suddenly
ketatamasíi	noisy, loud, shrill
béru	bell
otó	noise
nari-hazimeru	begins to ring
naru	rings, sounds
ryoogawa	both sides
nâku (= nâkute)	without there being (adverbial used for gerund)

tisoo o tábetari, utá o utattári, géemu o sitári site, tanó-
siku asobi, sitizi-hañ goro, miñna sorézore no uti e káette
ikimásita. Oñna no hito wa, miti ga kurái no de, hitoribítori otokó ga okutte ikimásita ga, Matuyama-kuñ ga Káttyañ o
otaku máde okutte ikimásita. Káttyañ no uti wa, watakusi no
uti kara, kurai Gósyo no yoko o tóotte ikánakereba narimaséñ.
Matuyama-kuñ to Káttyañ wa, tanósikatta koto nado hanasi-
nágara, makkura na miti o arúite imásita.
Suru to, totuzeñ, ketatamasíi béru no otó ga nari-hazime-
másita. Ryoogawa ní wa ié mo náku, totuzen, kurayami no náka
kara óoki na béru no otó ga kikoeta monó desu kara, hutarí
wa, kosi o nukasañ bákari ni odorokimásita. Omówazu, Káttyañ
wa "Kyáa," to oogóe o agetá kara tamarimaséñ. Motomoto Matuyama-kuñ mo kowagari no otokó desu kara, Káttyañ o hotte
oite, itimókusañ ni hasiri-dasimásita. Omáwari-sañ ga yatté
kite, iroiro to sirabemásita ga, ittai náñ no kotó ka, sap-
pári wakarimaséñ desita. Yokuyoku kañgáete miru to, Káttyañ
ga Kóobe kara motte káette kita kabañ no náka ni irete átta
mezamasi-dókei ga kabañ no náka de nari-dásita kotó ga wa-
karimásita. Kóobe o déru toki, isóide déñsya ni notta monó
desu kara, mezamasi-dókei no béru no naru botañ o tomeru
kotó o wasurete kabañ ni ire, sono mama sukkári wasurete itá
no desita. Omáwari-sañ mo, hutari no awatemono ni odoróite,
warainagara káette ikimásita. Matuyama-kuñ wa, mezamasi-
dókei no háitta Káttyañ no kabañ o ságeta mama, hasiri-
dásita no desita.
Sono hí wa, hutarí wa buzi ni kaerimásita ga, sore kara
noti, Káttyañ wa, dóo site mo, Matuyama-kuñ to issyo ni
kaeránaku narimásita. Odoróite Káttyañ o sutete oite, hasít-
te nígeta Matuyama-kuñ ni okutte morau gúrai nara, hitóri de
káetta hoo ga añsiñ ná no da soo desu.

Vocabulary for Exercise 23

yó (= yóru)	night
Yokota	(a family name)
-tyañ - (= -sañ)	Miss (familiar)
Káttyañ	(a girl's name)
sono koro (= sono goro)	at that time
ozisama (= ozisañ)	uncle
tetudáu	helps out
syuumatu	week-end
kita tokoro désita	
(= kimásita)	had come

18. Ya yu yo, ra ri ru re ro. Yokohama ya Kamakurá. Áme mo yukí mo hurimásita. Kumamoto kara Simonóseki e ikimásita. Rósiya to Sína. Háru ni wa iroiro na omosirói kotó mo arimasu.
19. Wa (wo =) o ñ, ga gi gu ge go, za zi zu ze zo. Watakusi wa sore o mimásita ga, wakarimaséñ. Giñkoo no migi no hóo ni wa eigákañ ga arimasu. Kono getá wa ikura gúrai simásu ka? Ohayoo gozaimasu. Gózeñ gózi ni ókita toki suzusíi to omoimásita.
20. Da (di =) zi (du =) zu de do, ba bi bu be bo, pa pi pu pe po. Tegami mo kozútumi mo dási ni ikimásita. Dóno tatémono ga giñkoo désu ka? Siñbuñ o yomimásita ka? Ano Beikokúziñ wa koñbañ sañpo ni ikimaséñ ka? Eñpitu wa ippoñ mo arimaséñ. Kippu wa náñmai irimásu ka?
21. Kya kyu kyo gya gyu gyo, sya syu syo zya zyu zyo, tya tyu tyo, nya nyu nyo, hya hyu hyo bya byu byo pya pyu pyo, mya myu myo, rya ryu ryo. Tookyoo kara Kyóoto made kisyá de ikimásita. Syúziñ wa byooki ni nátte syúzyutu-sarete kara, gyuunyuu o nomimaséñ. Otya wa dóo desu ka? Happyakú kara gohyakú o hiku to, sáñbyaku nokorimasu ne.
22. Watakusi wa Amerikáziñ no tomodati to issyo ni tiisái hóteru ni imásita. Teeburu no ue ní wa bíiru ga nihoñ arimásita. Sore o nóñde kara, náihu de páñ o kirimásita. Sore kara góhañ o tábete koohíi o nomimásita. Soo site, tomodati wa Surañsugo de "Tabako wa ikága desu ka" to iu to, watakusi wa "Hái, arígatoo gozaimasu. Mátti ga arimásu ka?" to kikimásita. Sono áto de hurúi zíipu ('jeep') ni notte doráivu ('drive') o site Nyuu-yóoku ('New York') ya Párii ('Paris') ya Róñdoñ ('London') no depáato ('department stores') no kotó o hanasimásita. Tomodati wa nakanaka rippa na sebiro o kite, zuboñ no pokétto ('pocket') ni mo uwagi no pokétto ni mo hañketi ('handkerchief') ga irete arimásita.
23. Áru yó no hanasí.
    Kyóneñ no áru hi no kotó desita. Yokota Káttyañ wa sono koro Kóobe no ozisama no ié e iroiro na kotó o tetudái ni itte imásita ga, syuumatu ni Kyóoto ni áru uti ni káette kita tokoro désita. Tokoro ga, tyoodo sono doyóobi no yóru, watakusítati no uti de haha no tañzyóobi no oiwai o suru kotó ni site imásita no de, Káttyañ o omaneki simásita. Sono hoka ní mo, Matuyama-kuñ ya Takagi-kuñ ya Yoshida-sañ ya Yasui-sáñtati mo kite imásita. Káttyañ wa zikañ ga nákatta tame, Kóobe kara tyokusetu ni watakusítati no uti e kabañ o ságete yatte kimásita. Go-

8. Ya yu yo, ra ri ru re ro. Hayái húne mo osoi húne mo mimásita 'We saw both fast ships and slow ships'. Áme mo yukí mo hurimásita 'Both rain and snow fell'. Yokohama ya Kamakurá. Kumamoto ya Simonóseki e ikimasu. Náni-ka arimásu ka 'Do you have something?' Háru, natú, áki, huyú. Rokú, sití, hatí. Rósiya to Sína 'Russia and China'. "Úmi" to iu ími 'the meaning "sea" '.

9. Wa (wo =) o ñ. Anó hito wa úmi o míta kotó wa arimaséñ. Watakusi wa wakarimaséñ. Íma wakarimásu ka? Warúi hito o míta kara, kaerimásita. Señtaku o sité kara, matí e arúite ikimásita 'After doing the laundry, I walked to town'.

10. Ga gi gu ge go, za zi zu ze zo. Náni ga arimásu ka? Giñkoo no migi no hóo ni wa eigákañ ga arimasu. Kono getá wa ikura gúrai simásu ka? Ohayoo gozaimasu. Kaze ga húite imasu ka? Gózeñ gózi ni ókita toki suzusíi to omoimásita. Húne ga sáñzoo arimásita 'There were three ships'.

11. Da (di =) zi (du =) zu de do. Hahá wa tegami o dási ni ikimásita. Kozútumi mo dásita ñ desu ka? Dóno tatémono ga giñkoo désu ka? Sóo desu ne.

12. Ba bi bu be bo, pa pi pu pe po. Obáasañ wa biñseñ o itímai motte imasu 'Grandmother has one sheet of stationery'. Siñbuñ o yomimásita ka? Ano Beikokúziñ wa mañnéñhitu o sañboñ motte imasu. Koñbañ sañpo ni ikimáseñ ka? Eñpitu wa ippoñ mo arimáseñ. Kippu wa náñmai irimásu ka?

13. Kya kyu kyo, gya gyu gyo, sya syu syo zya zyu zyo, tya tyu tyo, nya nyu nyo, hya hyu hyo bya byu byo pya pyu pyo, mya myu myo, rya ryu ryo. Ano kyúuzi wa kyóneñ Kyóoto kara kisyá de kimásita. Syokkoo to site, soko de hataraite imásita. Syúziñ wa syúzyutu-sarete kara, gyuunyuu sika nomimáseñ. Otya mo nomimáseñ ka? Byooki ni narimásita ka?

14. A i u e o, ka ki ku ke ko, sa si su se so. Áa. Íi. Ée. Áu. Aói. Oói. Ue. Ié. Iie. Káku. Éki. Koko. Késa. Siai. Sukósi. Séki. Sóo.

15. Ta ti tu te to. Na ni nu ne no. Atatakái. Tiisái. Tukue. Káite ita otokó. Sakana no sukí na néko to niku no sukí na inú.

16. Ha hi hu he ho. Hako wa ookíi ka, tiisái ka? Súihei wa húne ni itái ka? Hoka no heitai wa asoko e ikitái ka?

17. Ma mi mu me mo. Máiniti koko e kimásu ka? Náni-ka míte imasu ka? Samúi hi ni mo misé e ikimásu ka?

KEY TO THE EXERCISES

NOTE: For exercises consisting of a list of single words, and short phrases both romanization and meanings are given. For longer passages, only the romanization is given. The more difficult vocabulary items and a few grammatical points are presented separately after the text.

1. A i u e o. Áa 'ah!'. Íi 'It's good'. Ée 'Yes'. Áu 'He meets'. Aói 'It's blue'. Oói 'They are many'. Ue 'topside'. Ié 'house'. Iie 'No'.

2. Ka ki ku ke ko. Kao 'face'. Kau 'He buys'. Áki 'autumn'. Éki 'railroad station'. Oka 'hill'. Káku 'He writes'. Aku 'It opens'. Iku 'He goes'. Oku 'He puts'. Koko 'here'. Ookíi kí 'a big tree'. Iké 'pond'. Óke 'bucket'.

3. Sa si su se so. Sáa 'well!'. Ása 'morning'. Kása 'umbrella'. Sake 'rice-wine'. Késa 'this morning'. Saki 'ahead'. Kusa 'grass'. Siai 'match, (competitive) meet'. Usi 'cow'. Isu 'chair'. Sukósi 'a little bit'. Séki 'seat'. Sékai 'world'. Soko 'there'. Sóo 'It's so'.

4. Ta ti tu te to. Tasu 'He adds'. Takái 'It's tall'. Atatakái 'It's warm'.Ití 'one'. Tikái uti 'a house nearby'. Tiisái tukue 'a small desk'. Tutí 'earth, soil'. Kitá toki 'when he came'. Atúi koto 'being hot'. Káite ita otokó 'the man who was writing'. Asita ikitai 'I want to go tomorrow'.

5. Na ni nu ne no. Sakana no sukí na néko to niku no sukí na inú 'a cat that likes fish and a dog that likes meat'. Nani-ka íi 'something good'. Sono ue, náni-ka akai 'in addition, something red'.

6. Ha hi hu he ho. Hako no náka 'inside the box'. Ano hikóoki wa ookíi ka, tiisái ka? 'Is that airplane big or little?' Súihei wa húne ni itái ka? 'Does the sailor want to be on the ship?' Heitai wa koko e kitái ka? 'Does the soldier want to come here?' Hoka no heitai wa asoko e ikitái ka? 'Do the other soldiers want to go over there?' Hitótu, hutatú 'one, two'.

7. Ma mi mu me mo. Máiniti koko e kimásu ka? 'Do you come here every day?' Anó hito wa náni-ka míte imasu ka? 'Is he looking at something?' Samúi hi ni mo misé e ikimásu ka? 'Do you go to the store on cold days too?' Kimono mo kaimásita. 'I bought some clothes too.'

15

どはちじごろからいちじかんばかりのあひだきやうとのそらはまつかにもえ、まちぢゅうのひとぐ〜はこのひをみるために、まちのまんなかをながれてゐる『かもがわ』のかはらへでかけていきます。きやうとのひとだけではなく、このひにははるぐ〜おほさか、かうべはもちろんとうきやう、よこはまあたりからもこのうつくしいけしきをみに、たくさんのひとがあつまつてきます。にほんにゐるぐわいこくのひとにとつても、これはみのがすことのできないめいぶつのひとつです。

しのやまを『ひがしやま』、きたのやまを『きたやま』、にしのはうのやまを『にしやま』といひます。

まいねん、はちぐわつじふごにちにはこれらのやま〴〵になかたちのひがつくのでいうめいです。これはぶつけうのでんせつからきたもので、まいねんはちぐわつとをかごろからそれ〴〵のいへのごせんぞのたましひがふるいいへにかへつてきてかぞくといつしよにいつかのあひだゐることになつてをり、はちぐわつのじふごにちにふた〳〵びこれらのたましひはほとけさまのところへかへつていくことになつてゐます。このかへつていくたましひをおくるのが、このやま〴〵につく『おくりび』です。ひがしやまのなかのひとつを『だいもんじやま』といひ、ひやくメートルぐらゐのおほきさの『だい』のじのかたちにひをたきます。きたやまには『めうほふざん』といふやまがあり、妙法（めうほふ）といふやまのとほりにひをたきます。にしやまにもひとつ『だい』のじ、とりゐのかたちなど、みんなにふねのかたち、にしやまにもひとつ『だい』のじ、とりゐのかたちなど、みんないつ〳〵のじやかたちのひがいつせいにともされます。ひがにしやまにしづみ、ちやう

をうせい　こゑ　とうきゃう　かへる　わうじ　いへ　しゃうぐわつ　うゑき
じいう　こたへる　くわうこく　あふ　けふ　あらふ　とをか　あるきません
はづかしい　だらう　ゐる　まへ　ぢゃうぶ　しづか　つくゑ　くわじ　ちうもん
びゃうき　みづ　ぐわいこく　はなしませう　かはない　くらゐ　てぬぐひ
かひます　ちひさい　あをい　ゐど　をぢ　びんばふ　いきませう
みゃうにち　かはる　くわいしゃ　おもふ　をどる　たいね　いはない　いかう
かは　あへば　につくわう　おもふ　をどる　たらう　ぐわんじつ　をんな　かほ
はらふ　しほ　さうぢ　わらふ　ふぢゑ　きません　とぢる　やうか　いふ
まゐる　むかふ　をはり

27. 『きゃうとのおくりび』

きゃうとしはしはうをやまでかこまれてゐます。　ひがしがはにはさんじふろくのやま〴〵がずつとつゞいてをり、きたにもにしにもそれ〴〵やまがあります。　ひが

24. ゐゑを　くわぐわ　は　ひふへほ　ぢづ
ゐなか　ゐど　たいぬ　くらゐ　みる　こゑ　つくゑ　ゑん　つゑ　をとこ
をか　あをい　をんな　をどる　くわいしや　くわじ　ぐわんじつ　えいぐわ
かは　かはない　には　いはない　かはる　あひだ　ちひさい　かひます
てぬぐひ　あたひ　あふ　わらふ　はらふ　おもふ　あらふ　いへ　かへる　まへ
こたへる　あへば　かほ　やほや　なほす　いきほひ　にほふ　ぢしん　ふぢ
とぢる　みづ　しづか　はづかしい

25. とをか　おほかみ　おほかた　きのふ　やうか
だらう　はんたう　ぢやうぶ　くわうこく　むかふ　びんばふ　はふりつ
てふてふ　いきませう　けふ　しませう　ちうもん　いふびん　ほんしう

26. ゐなか　はふりつ　をとこ　つゑ　ゑん　くわし　まはり　めづらしい　なほす
すぢ　おほかた　てふてふ　おほかみ　きのふ　ぢしん　えいぐわ　ほんしう
いふびん　なんぢ　あたひ　しませう　やほや　れんしふ　には　いきほひ

わかりませんでした。よくよくかんがえてみると、カッチャンがコーベからもってかえってきたかばんのなかにいれてあったからだとわかりました。コーベをでるときいそいででんしゃにのったものですからめざましどけいのベルのなるボタンをとめることをわすれてかばんにいれ、そのまゝスッカリわすれていたのでした。おまわりさんもふたりのあわてものにおどろいて、わらいながらかえっていきました。まつやまくんはめざましどけいのはいったカッチャンのかばんをさげたまゝはしりだしたのでした。そのひはふたりはぶじにかえりましたが、それからのちカッチャンはどうしてもまつやまくんといっしょにかえらなくなりました。おどろいてカッチャンをすてゝおいてはしってにげたまつやまくんにおくってもらうぐらいなら、ひとりでかえったほうがあんしんなのだそうです。

ちそうをたべたりうたをうたったりゲームをしたりしてたのしくあそび、じゅうじはんごろ、みんなそれぐ〜のうちへかえっていきました。おんなのひとはみちがくらいので、ひとりぐ〜おとこがおくっていきましたがまつやまくんがカッチャンをおたくまでおくっていきました。

カッチャンのうちはわたくしのうちからくらいごしょのよこをとおっていかなければなりません。まつやまくんとカッチャンはたのしかったことなどはなしながらまっくらなみちをあるいていました。

すると、とつぜんけたゝましいベルのおとがなりはじめました。りょうがわにはいえもなくとつぜんくらやみのなかからおゝきなベルのおとがきこえたものですから、ふたりはこしをぬかさんばかりにおどろきました。　おもわずカッチャンは『キャー』とおゝごえをあげたからたまりません。もとく〜まつやまくんもこわがりのおとこですからカッチャンをほっておいて、いちもくさんにはしりだしました。おまわりさんがやってきていろ〜しらべましたが、いったいなんのことかサッパリ

23.
『あるよのおはなし』

　きょねんのあるひのことでした。よこた・カッチャンはそのころコーベのおじさまのいえへいろ／＼なことをてつだいにいっていましたが、しゅうまつにキョートにあるうちにかえってきたところでした。ところが、ちょうどそのどようびのよる、わたくしたちのうちで、は／＼のたんじょうびのおいわいをすることにしていましたので、カッチャンをおまねきしました。そのほかにもまつやまくんやたかぎくんやよしださんややすいさんたちもきていました。カッチャンはじかんがなかったためコーベからちょくせつにわたくしたちのうちへかばんをさげてやってきました。ご

ますか』とき＼ました。そのあとでふるいジープにのってドライヴをしてニューヨークやパリーやロンドンのデパートのことをはなしました。ともだちはなか／＼りっぱなせびろをきていて、ズボンのポケットにもうわぎのポケットにもハンケチがいれてありました。

21. キャ　キュ　キョ　ギャ　ギュ　ギョ　シャ　シュ　ショ　ジャ　ジュ　ジョ　チャ　チュ　チョ　ニャ　ニュ　ニョ　ヒャ　ヒュ　ヒョ　ビャ　ビュ　ビョ　ピャ　ピュ　ピョ　ミャ　ミュ　ミョ　リャ　リュ　リョ

トオキョオ　カラ　キョオト　マデ　キシャ　デ　イキマシタ。シュジン　ハ　ビョオキ　ニ　ナッテ　シュジュツ　サレテ　カラ　ギュウニュウ　ヲ　ノミ　マセン。オチャ　ハ　ドオ　デス　カ。ハッピャク　カラ　ゴヒャク　ヲ　ヒク　ト　サンビャク　ノコリマス　ネ。

22. わたくしはアメリカじんのともだちといっしょにちいさいホテルにいました。テーブルのうえにはビールがにほんありました。それをのんでから、ナイフでパンをきりました。それからごはんをたべてコーヒーをのみました。そうしてともだちはフランスゴで『タバコはいかがですか』といゝました。わたくしは『はい、ありがとうございます。マッチがあり

ヨコハマ ヤ カマクラ シモノセキ ヘ イキマシタ。アメ モ ユキ モ フリマシタ。ロシヤ ト シナ。クマモト カラ オモシロイ コト モ アリマス。ハル ニ ハ イロイロナ

19. ワ ヲ ン ガ ギ グ ゲ ゴ ザ ジ ズ ゼ ゾ
ワタクシ ハ ソレ ヲ ミマシタ ガ、ワカリマセン。
ノ ホオ ニ ハ エイガカン ガ アリマス。コノ ゲタ ハ イクラ グライ シマス カ。ギンコオ ノ ミギ
オハヨオ ゴザイマス。ゴゼン ゴジ ニ オキタ トキ スズシイ ト オモイマシタ。

20. ダ ヂ ヅ デ ド バ ビ ブ ベ ボ パ ピ プ ペ ポ
テガミ モ コヅツミ モ ダシ ニ イキマシタ。ドノ タテモノ ガ ギンコオ デス カ。シンブン ヲ ヨミマシタ カ。アノ ベイコクジン ハ コンバン サンポ ニ イキマセン カ。エンピツ ハ イッポン モ アリマセン。
キップ ハ ナンマイ イリマス カ。

アイウエオ カキクケコ サシスセソ
14. アア。イイ。エエ。アウ。アオイ。オオイ。ウエ。イエ。イイエ。カク。エキ。ココ。ケサ。シアイ。スコシ。セキ。ソオ。
15. タチツテト ナニヌネノ
アタタカイ。チイサイ。ツクエ。カイテ イタ オトコ。サカナ ノ スキ ナ ネコ ト ニク ノ スキ ナ イヌ。
16. ハヒフヘホ
ハコ ハ オオキイ カ、チイサイ カ。スイヘイ ハ フネ ニ イタイ カ。ホカ ノ ヘイタイ ハ アソコ ヘ イキタイ カ。
17. マミムメモ
マイニチ ココ ヘ キマス カ。ナニカ ミテ イマス カ。サムイ ヒニ モ ミセ ヘ イキマス カ。
18. ヤユヨ ラリルレロ

12. ばびぶべぼ ぱぴぷぺぽ おばあさん は びんせん を いちまい もって います。しんぶん を よみました か。あの べいこくじん は まんねんひつ を さんぼん もって います。こんばん さんぽ に いきません か。えんぴつ は いっぽん も ありません。きっぷ は なんまい いります か。

13. きゃ きゅ きょ ぎゃ ぎゅ ぎょ しゃ しゅ しょ じゃ じゅ じょ ちゃ ちゅ ちょ にゃ にゅ にょ ひゃ ひゅ ひょ びゃ びゅ びょ ぴゃ ぴゅ ぴょ みゃ みゅ みょ りゃ りゅ りょ
あの きゅうじ は きょねん きょうと から きしゃ で きました。しょっこう として、そこ で はたらいて いました。しゅじん は ぎゅうにゅう しか のみません か。びょうき に なりました か。ろっぴゃく に さんびゃく を たす と くひゃく に なります ね。

9. わ を ん
あの ひと は うみ を みた こと は ありません。わたくし は わかりません。いま わかります か。わるい ひと を みた から、かえりました。せんたく を して から、まち へ あるいて いきました。

10. が ぎ ぐ げ ご ざ じ ず ぜ ぞ
なに が あります か。ぎんこう の みぎ の ほう には えいがかんが あります。この げた は いくら ぐらい します か。おはようございます。かぜ が ふいて います か。ごぜん ごじ に おきた とき すずしい と おもいました。ふね が さんぞう ありました。

11. だ ぢ づ で ど
はは は てがみ を だし に いきました。こづつみ も だした ん です か。どの たてもの が ぎんこう です か。そう です ね。

6. そのうえ、なにか あかい。
はひふへほ
はこの なか。あの ひこうきは おおきい か、ちいさい か。すいへいは ふねに いたい か。へいたい は ここへ きたい か。ほかの へいたい は あそこへ いきたい か。ひとつ、ふたつ。

7. まみむめも
まいにち ここへ きます か。
か。さむい ひにも みせへ いきます か。きものも かいました。

8. やゆよらりるれろ
やゆよらりるれろ
はやい ふねも おそい ふねも みました。あめも ゆきも ふりました。よこはま や かまくら。くまもと から しものせきへ いきます。
なにか あります か。はる、なつ、あき、ふゆ。ろく、しち、はち。
ろしや と しな。『うみ』と いう いみ。

1. あいうえお
   ああ。いい。ええ。あう。あおい。おおい。うえ。いえ。いいえ。
2. かきくけこ
   かお。かう。あき。えき。おか。かく。あく。いく。おく。ここ。
   おおきい き。いけ。おけ。
3. さしすせそ
   さあ。あさ。かさ。さけ。けさ。さき。くさ。しあい。うし。すこし。
   せき。せかい。そこ。そう。
4. たちつてと
   たす。たかい。あたたかい。いち。ちかい。うち。ちいさい。つくえ。つち。
   きた。とき。あつい。こと。かいて いた。おとこ。あした。いきたい。
5. なにぬねの
   さかな の すき な ねこ と にく の すき な いぬ。なにか いい。

www.ingramcontent.com/pod-product-compliance
Lightning Source LLC
Chambersburg PA
CBHW071845290426
44109CB00017B/1927